I0162349

DARING DIVORCE

Navigating the Storm

STACEY DUCKETT

DARING DIVORCE

Navigating the Storm

STACEY DUCKETT

Copyright 2021 Stacey Duckett

All Rights Reserved.

All Rights Reserved. No part of this publication may be reproduced, distributed, or transmitted in any form or by any means, including photocopying, recording, or other electronic or mechanical methods, without the prior written permission from the author, except in the case of brief quotations embodied in critical reviews and certain other non-commercial uses permitted by copyright law.

First Printing: October 2021

ISBN–13: 978-1-7370634-1-4

BEEKEEPER PUBLISHING

A note to the Reader-Disclaimer:

This book does not intend to be a substitute for consultation with a professional healthcare provider or attorney. The publisher and the author cannot claim any responsibility for any loss or damage caused or alleged, directly or indirectly, by the information contained in this book.

About the Author

Stacey Duckett got married in 2000 and divorced in 2014 when her children were in the 2nd and 4th grades. When she realized it wasn't going to work out, she found the courage to pursue the challenge of seeking out a divorce. To say this book will make it easy would be a lie, but to say easier would be correct. Stacey has used the B.E.S.T. tips, and her ex and her cordially can meet together on occasions revolving around their children in a friendly manner. She has personally gone through a divorce and found a way to thrive from the storm. You can get through this challenging time too. She brings the readers advice from counselors, divorce attorneys, and tips from her very own Mom.

Stacey Duckett is a certified hypnotist, nutritionist, sleep coach, and chiropractic doctor in the health care field. She is also the author of Sensational Sleep.

She enjoys her two daughters, road trips, hiking, running while listening to audiobooks or podcasts, and a recent passion is attending toastmasters in her spare time. Stacey Duckett is available to speak at your upcoming event, please visit www.DaringDivorce.com.

Table of Contents

Table of Contents

CHAPTER 1

How Did You Get Here?

How in the HELL did you get here? Once upon a time it was "'til Death Do We Part" and now...SHIT has hit the fan, and you are getting a DIVORCE. Divorce wasn't the plan. What happened? You both said I do but now one of you – or possibly both – does not want the marriage anymore. When one is ready to move on, counseling to put you two together will not work. Both parties need to want to make it work. Maybe your relationship was great until you got married and started living with each other night after night. Maybe your relationship took its toll after you started having kids and you realized your values are not the same. Somewhere along the way problems began. Maybe a lack of respect started to occur, and you drifted apart. At least one of you is sick and tired of pretending that everything is okay when nothing is okay. You have less to agree upon and more items to complain about in your relationship. If you take an honest look, have you been shoving things under the rug?

Now that you are here –tossed amid the tumultuous waters of divorce – some reflection might help figuring out how to move forward. Take a minute to consider which of these situations describes why you got married:

- Was it just because the timing was right?
- You were of certain age tired of being single, and you wanted to have kids and thought, "Well, this person will do"?
- Were you head over heels for this person or did you marry because you felt obligated to marry this person?
- Did others tell you this is a good person for you to marry, so you did?

- Did you just assume that your values would match up when you have children but then realized your values did not match up? One wants the children to go to private school, do extracurricular activities, and perhaps the other did not. One believes in more structured discipline and the other in freestyle raising the children.

Did you recognize yourself in those reasons? If so, you need to examine whether the two of you have the ability to keep you together. It is my experience that pretending in a relationship is not okay as it eats away at your soul. How many of these qualities define your current marital experience:

- Do you have enough breathing room in your relationship?
- Do you feel like you are the parent of the other, not the mate?
- Do you feel like roommates, not soulmates?
- Are you sleeping with this person just to keep the peace?
- Do you have more respect for the prostitute because they are at least getting paid to

sleep with someone they don't necessarily want to sleep with, and you are not?

Ask yourself these questions. Time to be honest. Your time on this planet is ticking. At the end of your life, will you be wishing you had the courage to get the divorce and allow yourself to be happy? The polls on regretting divorce varies. Some examples of regretting the divorce could be from all the hassle of having 2 households, losing friends, giving up the married label, and less income. On the other hand, you could be extremely happy you got the divorce because you are happier on your own, you are no longer pretending but being authentically true to yourself. If you have requested the divorce and have some hesitation about getting a divorce and would like things to work out, then sure, give it another chance if it is possible – a counselor would be a great option. Regardless if you are the one requesting the divorce or not, getting to the point of not regretting it often relates to navigating the storm and making daily use of the B.E.S.T. tips in this book, even after the storm. Be busy by being productive. Expect Nothing. Sustain your real friends. Have tunnel vision.

Whether you initiated it or not, you will know when DIVORCE is the answer. For me, I was asked "What about the kids?" I asked myself, if my kids were in my shoes, would I want them to stay or divorce? The answer was I would like them to divorce if there was no chance it was going to work out. When you see the writing on the wall isn't blurry anymore, how could you stay? I wanted to show my daughters they can be strong women and can make a better life after divorce and be happy. If it comes to the point you are hanging in for the kids, what will you do later once they leave the house? Will you get a divorce once they are out? Adult children who hear about their parents getting a divorce often feel guilty that the parents stayed together because of them. It is regrettable if you wait to get a divorce to listen to your kids tell the both of you, "Why don't you guys get a divorce?" Is that what you are waiting for, your kids to ask you the questions you're too afraid to ask yourself?

That is what "a daring divorce" means – having the courage. If you can't stand a job, if you are not happy with your marriage, you show them to suck it up and hang in there because that is the right thing to do? B.S. If you ask me. People should be doing jobs they enjoy and be in happy marriages. There is no reason not to. Don't get me wrong, make it work and if it is not working, find out what does work. Life is for discovering yourself and how you can help yourself and others grow around you. Time is too precious to be wasting in doubt and insecurity. It might be that getting a divorce will help both you discover the real you.

Some people who are married and over the age of 50 think that their marriage is safe. Think again. Marriage for this age group, in particular, is on the rise. For the men of all ages, you should know that the wife requests over 70 percent of all divorces. My divorce was no exception. You see, for years, there was writing on the wall, but it was blurry. I could not read it, so I stayed in the marriage and gave it my all. One day, like so many, that request for the divorce was because someone did something, said something, or in my situation, asked in a heated discussion, "Do you want a divorce?" I had not thought about getting a divorce. All of a sudden it was like the optometrist adjusted the lenses and I could see the eye chart of the marriage read: It is NEVER going to work out.

All of a sudden, I felt a weight lifted off of my shoulders. The weight of pretending weighs quite a bit. It can take a toll on your health and well-being. When the weight came off my shoulders, I felt that I could breathe better.

Are you the one who requested the divorce? It might be a tad bit easier for you than the other, but it is still a difficult situation. If you are not the one requesting the divorce, but you are reading this book to find ways to get through this, the navigating tips will work for you too. You must first realize that divorce is very much like having a death in the family. You will go through these grief stages: **denial, anger, bargaining, depression, and acceptance.**

Denial after requesting a divorce can occur when the other party rents a 1-bedroom place. You might think when you have kids, "What are they thinking? How dare he or she get a one-bedroom when we have kids?" A lot of that is denial and/or saving money. They believe it is temporary! They think you will still get back together.

The next stage is **anger**. Don't be surprised about them badmouthing you to their relatives, friends, neighbors, anyone who will listen. Unfortunately, these comments can even be to your children. They start trying to build an army against you.

Next, they beg to try to work on it and get the other party to stay in the dead-end relationship. Think clearly about this. An example of **bargaining** is giving the soon-to-be-ex who is trying to bargain items on the list and telling them do these and we can consider going to a marriage counselor. When the bargaining comes, are you excited about making it work, or are you starting to hope the other person cannot live up to the bargaining requests?

You know it is over when you are not excited to make it work out when the thought of you getting stuck in the marriage with bargains puts a pit into your stomach. When deep in your soul, you are hoping he or she cannot come through with his or her promises so you can get out. The party that did not request the divorce might go through with some **depression**. If this is you, maybe you drink more or start drinking, maybe get a D.U.I. They begin to crumble. Unfortunately, some get stuck here for a long time. Hopefully, at some point, you will accept the situation and move on. Depression is tough. Please stop beating yourself up or the other one with emotional name-calling and blame.

Comparing you to these other couples who made it work, you may wonder, what is wrong with you or the other or both of you. There is not anything wrong with you. There was no mistake in marrying who you married. Some people married the one where it worked out well for them! Good for them. Going through a divorce was not a lesson their soul needed to learn. Be glad we have those couples on this planet that have fantastic relationships that you can aspire to-- for the next relationship. At the end of these stormy stages, the prospect of acceptance looms. But active work is required to achieve authentic acceptance. That is what the navigating tips in this book are designed to help you with. For now, your soul is going to get this spice of a daring divorce. If you use this ingredient wisely, you will be building fantastic character like none other. If you don't use it wisely, it will create havoc in many aspects of your life.

Let's face it: if both parties want a divorce, and there are no kids, it still isn't necessarily the easiest thing to do as your identities were presumably invested in this relationship with their partner and respective families. Certainly having kids adds more complexity to getting a divorce. Whether you are requesting the divorce OR not, if one doesn't want it and you have kids, it isn't a walk in the park. No, it is not like that at all. It is a storm. It is more like jumping off the ferry boat ledge during a storm from 6 feet above the water and into the Pacific Ocean. The freezing ocean. You don't get to walk down a ladder and tiptoe yourself in it. Nope. You will jump in, or one will push you in whether you like it or not. You will go down 6 feet before you come back up.

The water isn't tepid. The water is FREEZING! I can tell you how cold the water is, but it is colder than that. You should come prepared. You'll need two swim caps for the swim from Alcatraz to San Francisco, one a thermal cap to protect your head and another bright neon cap that goes on top, in case you go missing. It isn't a joke. Some people may go missing after requesting a divorce. You will want some goggles to keep the salt water out of your eyes. These items are like having a great counselor to protect your mind. You will want some wax or earplugs to protect you as well. It is like having an attorney who will tell you not to listen to what you hear from the other party and not speak something you shouldn't say. You will also want a wet suit that is thick enough to keep you warm but able to swim. These layers are the secrets to navigate the storm that will help you get through this daring divorce. Get your gear because if you are wise, you will find the shore instead of panicking and treading water, and you will start swimming right away. Yep, with sharks, jellyfish, ships, and other stuff lurking around and various currents too.

Why should you listen to me? To be honest, I was hesitant about writing about this topic and opening up to others about this subject. I have two daughters. What will they think? It has been several years since my divorce, and I am writing this subject with their approval. This subject popped into my head because I know that what I have discovered can help others. With over 50% of marriages ending in divorce, I know many would like some support in dealing with this experience. People going through a daring divorce are trying to figure out how to navigate through the storm. Look, I have been through a daring divorce, and I have also swum from Alcatraz to San Francisco. The B.E.S.T. tips are like wearing a wet suit. These tips I have put together have helped me make this transitional time more manageable and can help you. I am a certified hypnotist that knows the power of visualization can help to make changes occur. Plus, some tips for navigating the storm are given to me by my Mom. Yes, my Mom, the one who tried to talk me out of the divorce at first. Once she saw my reasoning, she did what she could to support me.

If you use the navigating tools, you will come out on the other side with more character. After going through the stages of denial, anger, bargaining and acceptance you will be able to make it to another stage, **thriving**. You will get through the divorce and if you have kids they will be more than just okay and will be able to thrive in their life. They will wonder in time how you ever stuck together and will often be weirded out at the thought of you ever getting back together. They will see in hindsight that you made the right decision. You will discover the real you, full of joy. You will realize life is better being true to yourself and each other instead of pretending. Turn to the next page to read the next chapter and learn about the navigating tips that will make your daring divorce easier.

CHAPTER 2

Tips that will Make Navigating the Storm Easier

C ome here, listen closely. You are jumping off of the ferry into the deep Pacific Ocean. In your ear, I will whisper the secret tips that you should employ to navigate your swim through the storm.

"You will need a thermal cap to protect your head, plus another neon color cap that goes on top-- in case you go missing, goggles to keep the saltwater out of your eyes, earplugs, and your wet suit."

The head caps keep your mind collected. The goggles are like having a great therapist to help keep your vision clear on future goals. The earplugs are like having a great family attorney who will tell you not to listen to what your spouse is about to say so you don't speak something you shouldn't say. People will say negative things and you could say things you might regret. You will most likely want a therapist and an attorney for at least a consultation and see if it is a good tailor for your wetsuit, your choices you make to protect yourself during the journey through the storm are a good fit. All of these components I consider the tools needed to help you navigate the storm. The B.E.S.T. tips on making your divorce easier that works for both parties:

Be Busy

Expect Nothing

Sustain Your Real Friends

Tunnel Vision for the Time Tunnel

Unlike signing yourself up for an Alcatraz swim to San Francisco, where you can take the time to train for it, in a divorce you typically won't have a lot of room to prepare before you take the plunge. You will need to be able to get yourself together and get your items. You will need to make it to the end of the swim through the storm on to land. Those who can gather the necessary resources faster will get through this easier and most likely quicker too. Maybe you are reading this and wondering how you are going to do this financially? Luckily, by preparing your equipment you don't have to weather the storm alone. It is important that you seek counsel from a family attorney and therapist because they can provide experience you lack and provide you with support. If money is not an issue, then get the ones highly recommend in your area. If money is an issue, there are resources in most communities. Contact your local bar association referral service and ask for an attorney specializing in family law that can help at a reduced fee. If you and your soon-to-be-ex can agree, you might be able to use an arbitrator at the courthouse. Many counselors are available at a reduced rate online, like the app *Talkspace Therapy and Counseling*. Unthinkable, but in the United States, 1 in 4 women and 1 in 7 men have been victims of severe physical violence by their partner in their lifetime. 1 in 15 children are exposed to intimate partner violence each year, and 90% of these children are eyewitnesses to this violence. If you are worried about your safety, you can call The National Hotline for Domestic Violence at 1-800-799 SAFE or visit hotline.org for help with domestic violence. As you read this you can see how important it is to gather your resources so you can get through your divorce.

The process of divorce can be daunting. But you can use the following tips to transform it into a daring one that positively shapes who you will become:

Be Busy by being productive. When I was going through my divorce, I was getting ready to run a marathon. I was involved in getting ready to be the president in a community club, running my own business, founder and race director for a local initial 5K event, and taking my kids to all of their school activities and extracurricular activities. I didn't just have one thing to focus on, the daring divorce. I had many things to place my focus on. Shortly after I met my therapist, I asked her if she thought it was terrible to have all of this on my plate while going through a divorce. She advised that the more you can balance on your plate, the better off you will be. She noted that those who have the most going on during this time can cope better. They take the divorce in bits and pieces. If you only have the divorce going on, then that occupies our mind in everything you do, think, and feel. Her comment sealed my resolve, and I added training for a triathlon, the Half Iron Man. While these particular activities might not be the most appealing or suitable in your case, best practice indicates that you should consider what are meaningful and enriching activities you can add to your plate. You see, divorce is like an onion. You will have to eat the entire thing. You can have it ALL by itself, and you will be a crying, sobbing mess. OR you can have it in bits and pieces like with a bowl of chili with a lot of ingredients. Adding that onion builds character in your chili, and you can build character in you too.

Expect nothing. This tip I got from my Mom. Expect nothing that way if you should happen to get anything, you will be pleasantly surprised. The fact is, if you could not get along when you were married, how in the hell do you expect to get along when you are divorced? There are no more bargaining tools. When you are married, you can get your spouse to do things simply because they don't want to hear the bitchin' or the prospect of withholding sex or whatever because one wants something for something. These transactional relationships can be as simple as "Hey, I will make your favorite dinner if you can just clean the garage." We have all done some bargaining after living together long enough. Some people get upset when the ex doesn't follow through with helping out with the kids. All of a sudden you hear, "I can't do this," or "I can't do that." It is as if they purposely want to make your life hellish because you are the one asking for the divorce. Maybe they are. Who cares? You could easily be bothered by this and rant about what this person didn't do and should have done. Hearing my Mom say the words "EXPECT NOTHING" loud and clear has stuck with me. It is much better to be pleasantly surprised when they do something to help you out versus being upset all the time because they did not do what you wanted them to do. Unless the other party is unsafe to have as a parent, having shared custody is most likely the best scenario. Once again, however, don't be surprised if you are the one asking for the divorce if the kids are more often with you or eventually with you all the time. Trust me when I say it is the other parent's loss. When I say expect nothing, this also means finances too. Do not confuse this with don't ask. Ask for all you want. I am just saying be prepared or start getting the skills to be ready that push comes to shove, you can sustain your household financially all by yourself. Yes, it is difficult. It is easier said than done, but you will figure it out. If your kids are still in elementary school or younger and you have no family support nearby, you will wonder how you did it, especially if your kids are still in elementary school or younger and have no family support because they don't live near you. I am telling you, that if you gather the gear needed for the storm, you too can do it. We will talk more about this in a later chapter.

Sustain Your Real Friends. You will find that the friends you made before your marriage are gold.

The friends you made while married when they find out you are getting a divorce may not be there like they use to be there for either of you. Maybe it is because they are worried it is contagious, wondering if they are next, or perhaps they just do not know who to invite over. If you have a lot going on for yourself and are attractive too, they may be insecure and worried about you getting involved with their partner. You may never know what the reason is for them abandoning your friendship. Who knows, and who cares what their reasoning is? Let them do what they feel they need to do to keep themselves in their perfect – and, for some, their pretend "ideal" – marriage. Some may stick or reach out to you later if they end up getting a divorce themselves. Take this time to reach out to your friends, make some new ones, and keep yourself busy with being productive, so you have something more to talk about than the damn divorce.

Tunnel Vision for the Time Tunnel. Going through a daring divorce is like going through a time tunnel. At first, you are going about your normal, daily routine. Then, life starts spinning out of control. To not get dizzy, you should look at the end of the tunnel. Instead, some people go through the tunnel looking too much to the same side. They start to spin and end on the other side like a corkscrew. They finally make it out dizzy and shattered but are done with the event. Like swimming from Alcatraz to San Francisco, a swimmer who does not swim efficiently will get tossed and turned and will have to travel longer distance to get back on course to swim to land. Others, unfortunately, look to one side of the tunnel and spin like a rat in a rat wheel. They keep turning but never get anywhere. Suppose you see this happening to a friend, share this book with them.

What do you need to do? Stop for a moment. Fix those goggles by taking time to review your goals. Put the earplugs in so you can stay focused on your course, put the caps on so you can stay calm. Is your wet suit zipper up entirely, are you busy with your own hobbies? Are you living in the past or living in the future? Are you having a hard time accepting what is? If you do not accept what is, you will go into a spin cycle. You will deny it, think it is only temporary, worry about it, replay it, act like a victim, blame others, be moody and depressed. You do not need to be like this. Accepting what is allows you to be open to new possibilities. Accepting what is will give you peace and help you get through the challenges of your divorce. Accepting opens your eyes to what you can do to live presently and start your future instead of wasting your time, your friends' time, and counselor's time on bickering and resisting what is happening.

To help you accept what is happening, take a good look at your role in this and the other's role—no need to condemn yourself or the other person. Just simply acknowledge why this is happening. How would you like things to be different? Acknowledge the potential disconnect between what you would like and what the other wants. Yes, it sucks if one wants to stay married and the other one does not want it. But, acknowledge that this is what it is, and you cannot change the other person. You've gotten to this point and accept this isn't going to work out, so what can you do now? You can make this a daring divorce by starting your discovery into what you would like to do and to create, and how you want your life to be in the future.

Look at the B.E.S.T. tips, your secret to navigating the storm that will make your divorce easier. Ready or not, it's time to jump in.

CHAPTER 3

How to Do a Daring Divorce

This book can't answer should you be getting a divorce. If you are not sure, reach out to your counselor. If you are the one who wants the divorce, you may have people around you – even family members – that do NOT support your decision. You need to do what is suitable for you and your children. You need to do what is ideal for you and your children. Do you want to wait until your kids are begging you to get a divorce? This read is for those who know they are getting a divorce. This book is specifically about how to get through the divorce emotionally. For the ins and outs of how you can get by without a divorce attorney and how to go about it if you need one, I recommend the book *How to Make Any Divorce Better* by Ed Sherman, an attorney with over 40 years of experience. To tell you how to when I am not an attorney, and when each state has a different set of rules, I couldn't justify expanding in this area. There are also plenty of YouTube videos you can search for that will be helpful using keywords such as divorce in and the name of your state, "how to get a divorce in Texas" for example, or when you need a divorce attorney in Texas. You will need to find out if this is contested or uncontested. Hopefully, it will be uncontested since if both parties want the divorce and can verbally agree, it won't be as difficult. When it is contested, a concern can be you and your children's safety. Sometimes the other party will not make it easy for you when they do not want a divorce.

Using mediation is a great tool. However, there are times you will want to have an attorney. If you are busy with work and activities and want to make sure the papers will be complete correctly, you will need to figure out which experts can help you develop a successful plan: attorney, a mediator, or if you are doing it yourself. Then, follow through with the plan. If the other party is stalling, consider reaching out to an attorney.

Divorces can take many different forms such as

- Both parties want it and can come to an agreement on their own
- Some may not like the divorce but will do their best to make a smooth transition instead of complete nonsense and tragedy. They are smart enough to want to just get to the end of the tunnel.
- Some will swim with current against them in the storm.
- Some will not only have a current but someone on a kayak with a belt around you and be going the other direction.

Suppose both parties can be reasonable in a calm manner – fantastic! When you can't agree, consider an attorney, especially when you are simply not getting anywhere with your wanted divorce. That is like treading water forever but not getting anywhere. Don't you want to get to land?

Once you have decided whether you will use an attorney or not, next consider all of the assets and child custody. Most will want shared custody. Each state may be different, so it is crucial to consult an advisor in your state. When you are going through a difficult time, such as a divorce, you will do better if you can maintain being busy by being productive. If your soon-to-be-ex had an affair and trust is gone and you are requesting the divorce or even if they are requesting the divorce it will be best for you to keep in mind this person isn't right for you any longer. It doesn't mean that there is something wrong with them or with you. Look, maybe your values and their values do not match up. Perhaps they put a restraining order on you or tried to make you look bad in front of your family, and it wasn't deserving. Maybe they, too, were upset and felt unsafe and justified in doing what they did to you. Do your best to stay calm. You will be able to get through this by praying for them, for yourself, and for your kids to be happy, safe, and feel loved; having mantras and keeping busy will help you.

Do you want to hang on and be with someone who doesn't want to be with you? Do you want to go through life pretending? Life is excellent, and there is no reason to have to compromise on your values. Life is about discovering you. If you and your partner are not growing together but growing away, isn't it about time to wake up and see what is going on? Seek out your real friends. Spending time with friends that were your friends before the marriage is usually a safe bet. Making new friends is great too, perhaps from a new meetup group or a community club.

Finally, staying focused on the end game will work as a single parent if you have children. Make a list of all the items, chores, your soon-to-be-ex does to help around the house. Look at the list. Once the divorce is final, who will do these items on your list? Will it be you, someone you hire, or will you get your children to help? It is very likely you will be doing these chores so start practicing now. Or perhaps it will be your child's new chore to do to help out. For instance, I think he should take out the garbage, bring in the groceries, cut the lawn, etc. I put the kids on with chores, and I started mowing the lawn. I couldn't figure out how to get the lawnmower to start with so much effort. I got those push lawn mowers and got a great workout. I eventually got tired of it and found a landscaper to come over and take care of it. Maybe at times, you can hire a handyperson. Maybe learn more YouTube D.I.Y. videos. Get ready. You are going to learn a lot more. Learn perhaps how to fix the garage door or maybe learn a new recipe. If extra money is going to be needed which is most likely for most, consider downsizing. Maybe that garage sale. Have your kids learn how to sell the items they no longer use at the garage sale or sell it online. Going through the divorce, you may think the other party should do this or that but remember, EXPECT NOTHING. If you go through with the attitude of I got this and prepared for taking care of items without this party in the picture, you will be much calmer and be more at ease. So if the other party does help you out, excellent, that is a blessing.

You will learn to become more self-reliant and, with that, build more skills and confidence. My daughter at the time was taking harp lessons. Her Dad would have been the one to figure out how to string an instrument and tune it. With him out of the picture, I was able to pay attention enough to watch a video on YouTube and follow the instructions her teacher gave me. At a Christmas party after the divorce, all of the family and friends in attendance were amazed that Stacey could tune the entire harp when the string popped.

Figuring out how the everyday aspects of life are going to work will make the journey a whole lot easier. My kids were in activities where I would count on the spouse to pick them up if I was working. I rearranged my schedule so that I would be able to pick them up. Did it affect my finances? Perhaps it did. Being self-employed, I was fortunate that I was able to arrange my schedule as I saw fit. I have enjoyed being there for my girls and working and thankfully supporting all 3 of us. If you have activities that you find you are just not going to afford right now or can't find the rides because you work, then discover what activities you can do with them. If there is a will, there is a way to be involved in making it work. Think about your family traditions. Will you be able to keep them, or will you need to make new ones? My family lives away from us, but my ex's family is nearby. I was fortunate that I could continue having my girls involved in get-togethers at holidays and special occasions. Will this be the same for you? If not, have them look forward to a new tradition. Perhaps it will be camping and a road trip over their birthdays or spa day during Thanksgiving. If difficult to afford a spa day at a resort, consider having your special spa day right at home. If you have boys, think about a sports fest day or maybe a music day if your kids are into it. The point is to discover who you are and who your kids are and what they love to do.

Going through a divorce is difficult, especially for your kids. Getting your kids in counseling and helping them see they are not alone is a normal, even invaluable endeavor. Having them see options where they can still have great relationships with both Mom and Dad and do not need to take sides is the best for kids.

When getting a divorce, it is not uncommon for the party who does not want the divorce to accuse you of wrongdoings, say not such lovely things, and try to make you look bad in front of your children. Sad. Remember what an attorney and a counselor would most likely tell you. Stay calm and refrain from retaliating as it just fuels the fire. When the other party sees that they can't get a reaction from you, get ready. They may try to get a response from your children. Now I will admit that I would get more than upset when this happened to me – a conversation ending in a heated argument. Your kids see this, and once they know that you are not going to tolerate it, they will process how this party treated you. Unfortunately, the ex may start treating the child the same way trying to get a reaction. The ex may only treat one child this way because one child can more easily stop this nonsense with his/her demeanor, where the other may be too eager to try to make the parent happy. Happiness doesn't come from someone else.

Reassure your children that you love them. Get them the support that they need as often as they need it. If you can show that you just let what this person says go in one ear and out the other with not once flinching, they will see it and perhaps learn to do the same when needed. I have one daughter that tends to internalize and interpret hurtful things and another daughter who won't tolerate it and doesn't let it upset her. Each child has a way of coping with the stress of divorce. Checking consistently on your children is crucial to helping them overcome the obstacles they may face.

When I went through the divorce, many people in my life were not at first supportive, which was okay as it just made me confirm that I made the decision. Expect the naysayers maybe because of religious sentiments that frown upon divorce, or other people projecting their fear of the unknown, or some because they just want you to stay in the same dilemma. Reaching out to others who have already gone through the divorce process can be comforting. People who are strong in their marriage will still be there and will be supportive.

Think about joining some community groups or getting involved in meeting new people. Going through this divorce with a positive attitude, although challenging, will build your character. This life is an adventure, and what an adventure. You believed in happily ever after, but if you are reading this book, then was it? Some things are not forgivable, and if it has come to that, how could you stay? Ideally you can let bygones be bygones and take the best that came from the relationship and be thankful for what you learned from that time together. I am so ever grateful to God that I have two beautiful children. What a blessing it is to have them in my life. I am blessed to have gotten the opportunity to be their Mom. I learn from them, and they learn from me, and we have an excellent relationship.

You too can apply these tips for your daring divorce. Be busy by being productive. Find ways to keep you busy such as how to financially support yourself, keeping you active with some sort of exercise, some activities that help get your mind off of the divorce such as doing some form of art or playing an instrument. Expect nothing. Sustain your real friends and have tunnel vision through this challenge. Going forward, enjoy reading about the B.E.S.T. tips in more detail. First, let's start with being purposefully busy.

CHAPTER 4

Why Should You Be Busy Multitasking?

Be busy. I thought multitasking was a sure way not to get ahead. In some instances, that may be true but let me assure you that most likely is not the case. If your focus is constantly overwhelmed in the gut-wrenching and painful details of the divorce, you will find it challenging to navigate this storm. Your day will tend to be full of angst. You will feel eaten up from the inside out. The storm of the divorce will consume you! However, if you have many pieces that make up your activities, then the divorce will be only a part of it. If the divorce seems to be consuming all of your thoughts, then make parts of your life with more activities and deadlines. You may find that divorce goes from occupying all of your time to just a 1/4 of your time. If you make yourself even busier than before, perhaps you can get it to 1/8 or even 1/16th of your pie. Wow! That would be fantastic. You will still have to process it all, but it does not affect you as much as if it was the entire thing on your plate. It is that simple. Remember I talked about an onion being like a divorce? You will have to eat the whole thing. If you eat the onion all by itself, you will be a crying, sobbing mess. Do you want a bowl full of onions or chili with a lot of stuff in it with bits of onion on the top that creates character? For me, I will take the bowl of chili any day.

Having tasks that have deadlines helps you focus on that specific task at hand, giving you a break from the other job of dealing with the storm. Having another focus forces you to clear your mind. It will help you later address the sometimes unpleasant but necessary aspects of the divorce more clearly. It also allows you to start focusing on what other items you have on your plate with deadlines. Just multitasking alone can lead to cognitive overload because you are merely switching back and forth your attention but multitasking with deadlines is key.

What should you include in your tasks? Cardiovascular activity. Exercises activate your brain's frontal lobe, helping you manage time and memory. It allows the release of cellular growth factors. As a result, you will be able to handle two tasks better compared to doing one job alone. Processing decisions while exercising helps one be more efficient with exercising. If you are the one who does not want the divorce, getting physically active is more important than ever – maybe making you feel better because you look better and providing more personal satisfaction.

Learning something new requires you to focus on something else. The neuropathways built during the learning of a new task creates strong links with your current "sense of self" while decreasing the chains of divorce on your present identity. Instead of riding the merry-go-round repeatedly with all of your thoughts, you will have new input that requires you to focus elsewhere. The stronger you build this connection, the less spinning you will endure on the merry-go-round, even to the point you can get off of the merry-go-round and be an observer versus being on it. Learning something new can be meditative and help you to accept what is going on. Fun, enriching activities that can occupy your mind and develop a stronger sense of self include learning how to knit or learning to play an instrument or a new card game. You could also learn a new skill like golfing or tennis. It is time for you to discover your passions. What strikes your curiosity? What is it that you like? Gardening? Join a gardening club. Do you want to volunteer? Consider joining your local Rotary Club. Do you enjoy speaking? Maybe join your local Toastmasters Club. All of these activities help to keep your brain sharp. Neurogenesis is a process of the growth of new cells that occur throughout your life at all ages. Learning something new changes your brain.

Being involved helps protect you. Your passion might include learning to play the piano, learning a new language, writing, playing chess, or taking a cooking lesson. By trying new things, you might find very often one you like more than another. The point is to keep learning and discover yourself if you do not know what to pick, something that fits your schedule, and then stick with it. It is okay to try something and find out it is not for you – you have the opportunity to be daring and keep looking for something you do enjoy.

If you can pick up that habit of doing meditation, that is great. I know that during a time like this, it is challenging. You try to sit still but then your mind starts going straight to thinking about the divorce. Many people think of meditation as sitting still but meditation can also be in the form of art like knitting or painting as it helps you to be more present and focus your mind by taking you to another step outside of yourself. Creating art is beautiful. Instead of repeatedly going with the same thoughts, it enables you to focus on something else. Enjoy time creating a piece of your self-made art. Creating art or music helps you take a break from everything else that is going on, it is like a mini vacation helping you deal with stress.

If you have enough items on your plate keeping you busy with deadlines and just a tiny portion for you to focus on the divorce, you will be able to sleep at night. If you are not sleeping well, ask yourself if you have enough going on. If not, ask yourself, should you be doing more right now? If you feel you have more than enough going on and are still having difficulty sleeping, check out my other book *Sensational Sleep, Better Sleep for a Better You.* You are going to want sensational sleep for this Daring Divorce. Sleep is an essential tool for you to navigate the storm. Having both sleep quality and quantity will help you with clarity, help you be less anxious and depressed, and put you in a better mood. Proper sleep helps restore your body and mind and get you prepared for the day.

Let's make a checklist and see what you have on your plate to see if you have enough going on.

Do you have some form of exercise on your plate? Cardiovascular and some form of resistance training? Those who physically take care of themselves feel better. Don't you want to feel more attractive?

Do you have something new to you on your plate? Like dancing a contemporary dance, taking up a sport you never played before, or learning a musical instrument?

Do you have something creative on your plate? Like knitting, journaling, painting, or sculpting?

Do you have something you are doing that is passively taking care of yourself? Like getting a massage, pedicure, manicure, getting your beard trimmed, or a new hairstyle? Maybe it could be as simple as having an afternoon tea and taking a nap on your hammock outside. When was the last time you took a road trip to someplace new? Perhaps to the ocean or park and gathering in some sunshine. Gathering sunshine can help increase serotonin levels, boost your mood, and help your internal clock turn the melatonin on at night to help you fall asleep. Get some sun into your life to help you navigate the daring divorce storm.

Keeping your kids busy, if you have any, is key to helping them as well. Just do not let their activities be the only thing you focus on. They have their life and you have yours independently from each other. They need to see you also have your hobbies around you.

Expecting yourself or your soon-to-be-ex handle the expenses of two households at your current lifestyle may not be possible. Your living standards might change quite a bit. Moving into an apartment from a four-bedroom house can be difficult, or it can be liberating. I found downsizing liberating. You are getting rid of all this stuff that accumulated throughout the years. Now, I make it a continued practice to weed through items that do not have a purpose for our household and give them to someone who can use those things. Spend some time cleaning up. Maybe you need to have a garage sale. Perhaps this is time to look at what kind of career you like to have and what side hustle you can muster. Do you have the skills or need to take some classes to have the proper training? Do you like floral arranging? Perhaps you could work in a floral shop and eventually get your own business going. Maybe you want to get into real estate. You can take classes online and study for them and start working. There are endless pursuits.

Lastly, another thing that might seem inconceivable to even consider at this moment is dating. It is only natural to seek companionship. If you continue to work on the B.E.S.T. tips and develop yourself, then you may find that area wanting. After six months to a year, you might consider dating others if your divorce is not final. For some, you may want to wait longer. Dating when the divorce isn't final might strike a chord with the religious right. Why? I know some examples where the divorce is still held up in court five years later. Are you going to keep your life on hold? I am not saying you have to sleep with anyone. I am just saying going out to meet others can help you feel some excitement and realize there are options. If you are not comfortable with dating, think about joining a meetup group for some social atmosphere You will notice you have more enthusiasm about taking care of yourself and enjoy the full benefits of looking your best. You will see there is light at the end of the tunnel. Just keep it light. What is the best way to get a lot of dates? Online dating. There are numerous free ones and paid ones. I know you can find the right one for you. Keep your photo updated and keep your profile light, nothing too heavy, and for Pete's sake, don't talk about your divorce. When they speak, listen. It might give you some insights. By the way, many, if not all of your married friends, will look at you with envy. Enjoy this part of it.

In the next chapter, we will discuss expecting nothing. That means get yourself ready to support yourself if you are not doing so already.

CHAPTER 5

Why Should You Expect Nothing?

Perhaps you never worked, or you decided to stay home once you started having kids. Maybe you worked hard to help your-soon-to-be-ex go to school. You feel you are entitled to alimony. Maybe. Every state is different. It may depend on how long you were married and the prospects of you getting back into the workplace. It may just come down to what the judge says. Your attorney can get you the real scoop about what you can get for alimony, let alone child support. However, I think you must have a reality check.

I was going on and on to my Mom, "He should do this, and he should do that, but he isn't, Mom. Can you believe it?" People and friends don't want to hear it. They have their crap. Some aren't as fortunate as you. Some would love to leave their marriage, but they do not have the audacity, the strength, or the courage to do a daring divorce, so they continue as is, stagnant. You are the one who is going to have a significant change, and you can take it and make it build you or tear you apart. The choice is yours. Others may have a great marriage, good for them. Something perhaps to aspire to in your future.

When I was bickering, my Mom stopped me and gave me some advice: "If you did not get along when you were married, how do you think you will get along once you are divorced?" There are no more bargaining tools. **Expect nothing** sure beats being upset all of the time. You can go on and on about all the things this person should be doing, but it is pointless and a waste of time. I did not say you don't ask for anything. Ask for all you want. I am just telling you don't expect anything. My Mom had a point; this way, you will be pleasantly surprised and have a better mood if you do get anything. It will make your divorce and life after the divorce easier. Your plan A – "marry to death do us part" – did not work, so get your plan B and get ready. Learning to be self-sufficient will build your confidence and make you more appealing than you already are.

In the last few decades, women increased their schooling and went to work to help the household out. I do not think it was to let the other half take a back seat and let one do the household chores, take care of the children, and work while the other sits on the couch all day, for instance, and plays video games. Nowadays, depending upon where you live, both partners work to pay the monthly expenses to operate. Now with a divorce, perhaps you won't be going out to eat all of the time. Get your crockpot out. Kids will come home and smell the wonderful aroma and know you care about them. If you have a picky eater and the kids are old enough, they will learn how to make themselves something to eat to nourish themselves. When you expect nothing from your ex, you can expect your children at a certain age to help with doing the laundry, cleaning up, taking out the trash, and maybe even cutting the lawn. Take your list out you made from chapter 3 and consider how you can divvy up the tasks.

You may find some work you can do from home online while your kids are home. Don't feel guilty if you need to pawn your wedding ring if you need money for food. Nourishment and a roof over your head are more important than a pretty ring.

Most people would love to play the lottery and have all of their numbers show up. Have you won the lottery? Maybe you will get everything you ask for, but you should not expect it. I cannot tell you enough how vital it is that both boys and girls get an education or get trained in a trade. Having the ability to have your income take care of yourself and your children and to be able to leave a potentially unsafe marriage is essential. Do you want your daughter or son to be stuck in a marriage that is unhealthy or unsafe? It is difficult to divorce if you do not have the financial resources. Perhaps you think my soon-to-be-ex-spouse should pay you alimony and child support. Maybe the judge will agree with you but maybe not. The soon-to-be-ex-spouse could claim he has a disability and can't work as he did, or they can get their boss to pay them under the table. There are so many ways for them to hide their money. Instead of wasting time trying to find out where it is hidden, invest in yourself to get the training you need to get ahead of the game. You will feel better about yourself and more confident. Some will tell you that you are entitled to child support, but if your soon-to-be-ex is self-employed, they have a way to hide it. Is it worth your time and effort getting a private eye to investigate for you, or more money spent on an attorney, or would that money be better for you to use on your education? It is more challenging to get someone to pay for their child support than you would think in many cases. You would think they would want to contribute to their children's well-being, but unfortunately, your soon-to-be-ex might prioritize selfishness and self-conservation. They may rather spend money on a new love going on lavish vacations instead of taking their kids to a unique resort. All the stuff you would have like to have done they can now do all of a sudden without a care in the world. On the days they say they will have the kids for shared custody, they may decide not to be available.

When you expect your ex to do everything you want them to, you may find that you are often frustrated. Your ex might not help out how you like. Do you want your children to see you upset, or would you prefer them to see you happy and surprised and more on the side of being appreciative when your ex does something you want them to do?

It is not as easy as it sounds, but ask for whatever you like from your ex but expect nothing from your ex. You will find yourself less disappointed and in a better mood if your ex turns out to do most of what you agreed to be thankful for. If your kids see you be graceful, they may be able to learn to be appreciative.

Some who are getting a divorce have to continue to live in the same household, which isn't very easy. How can one start to recover if one can never have some space to get some clarity? There are many ways nowadays one can begin to earn an income. It is essential to discover your unique talents. Then find work where you can utilize your gifts. You can do a short survey https://www.*viacharacter.org*, and you will get a list of your top talents. There is also a cool tool at *https://www.mynextmove.org* that shows your aptitudes and suggests some potential careers and even shows potential jobs locally. See how you can use these in a job you might like to do. If you have your own business already and will know you will need more money, think of what else you could incorporate into your business to make more income. Or is there some side hustle you can do? It would be best if you also prepared yourself. If your ex picked up the children and took them to their extracurricular activities, they may now be reluctant to do so, making the kids suffer. How are you going to make it work? Be prepared. Your ex might not be okay with paying for the kids' activities they have done all along if it requires money. They may say no, it isn't necessary. If you want them to go, you may have to pay for it and get them there. I hope that is not the case for you, but I have heard of that happening way too often. What kind of support do you have with grandparents if kids are little? I know my kids were in the second and fourth grades when I decided we would be getting a divorce. My Mom was going to move out and stay with me in California to help me. Ended up, she did not come out. I was a bit stressed, thinking about how I would swing it. But I did. The time flew by, the kids became old enough, and I somehow managed to make it work. It did help that my office was right next to their school. It did help the fact I have my own business and scheduled my hours around their extracurricular activities. Was it difficult? Yes. I do believe if there is a will, there is a way. Occasionally you may have to ask for a friend's help or a relative. Figure out your plan on how to survive if your ex agreed to nothing. You can make it work. Things will change. Your kids might even learn to help out a little more too. Maybe your vacations will change to something not so far away or expensive. Kids just want to spend time with you wherever you visit.

Going through a divorce will require you to scrutinize your expenses. You need to have a plan when you expect nothing. Some important areas to budget for include:

- Mortgage or rent
- Car
- Child care
- Food
- Gas
- Health Insurance
- Life Insurance
- Children's activities
- Your activities/Gym Memberships/ Organizations
- Pet Care
- Utilities
- Wardrobe
- Subscriptions
- Prescriptions
- Birthday Gifts
- Holiday Gifts
- Entertainment
- Taxes
- Other such as travel, dry cleaning, lawn services
- Savings

What is your budget? Is it possible you can live with a family member until you get enough income to take care of your family? When you make your income, you will feel more confident and be more appealing to everyone. How can you save money? OR how can you make more money? Or a bit of both. I used to get brand new clothes for my kids, and now occasionally, I still do. But you know what my kids love? To earn their own money and go thrift shopping. I have to admit they have gotten some excellent picks. They have also learned how to repurpose items, take things they don't have, and sell them. Did you notice that I put savings in there? If you do not put it in your budget or do not have it automatically done, it often doesn't get done.

We got rid of cable and the T.V. Do you need to get a less expensive but working car? Are you paying for a storage unit? Start a garage sale or sell items online. When I was going through the divorce, I sold things and realized I was making several hundred dollars, so I immediately went back inside the house and started selling everything we no longer had use for or a place for them. I could then donate everything else and get a tax deduction. How cool is that? Save on the darn storage fees. Why are you waiting? Do you even know anymore what is in there? Maybe some items are sentimental? Take a photo of them, then sell the items if you need money. We have the computer of course with WiFi and found that to be more than enough for our busy schedules. How often do you go out to eat? Is it too often? Maybe we could change that to some more homemade dinners and breakfasts where the kids learn to help, and perhaps when old enough, they can start making some dinners. Having an accountability partner for your spending is ideal. Using QuickBooks may help you see where you are spending your money so you can make better decisions. Don't have the budget for QuickBooks? Try nerdwallet.com or pocketguard.com; both are free apps.

Some benefits of downsizing are you stop playing the game of always trying to have the perfect everything. Downsizing from all of the items you have collected in your household that you rarely use is like getting rid of flotsam and jetsam and keeping just the buoys you need to guide you to the end. You can stop trying to keep up with the Jones family down the street. As you clear your space and start living more on purpose and less clutter, you will begin to grow and build more internal character. You can relax and enjoy what you do have. If the kids end up with you all of the time even though there is supposed to be shared custody, eventually, you will see who the kids favor.

Developing yourself through education and taking care of yourself will help you become more appealing than you already are. Not relying on someone else builds you up, and you will inspire your children. Maybe you won't be getting your nails done for a while or shopping in the fancy stores. Learn to appreciate what you do have and learn to make it work with accessories. Make your own money, and you can spend your own money. If one earns all the money, how does the other feel? Like a kid asking for a few dollars for candy all of the time?

Check your credit and look at each account. You can go to Experian.com for a free report. Is anything in both of your names and has recently gone up in charges? If you have joint accounts, call to get your name off or not allow anymore to be charged. If you do not have a savings account for emergencies, you know why they are good to have. Start one if you haven't as soon as you can put funds in there.

If you were the wife and stayed at home and did not work during this time taking care of kids, getting financing up to speed is critical. You should know that women spend approximately a decade or less at work, typically because of childrearing. To this year, 2021, women generally make less than men for the same job. Therefore, women usually don't have as much money saved or invested for retirement or emergency funds. It would be best if you thought about how you can be prepared for years ahead of you, let alone getting through this daring divorce.

So far you realize that **being busy** with productive activities will help you keep your mind focused on being in the present versus being out of control. **Expecting nothing** from your soon-to-be-ex will help you become self-sufficient and bring an appreciation for anything your soon-to-be-ex does that is helpful. For many the need to find additional income will be an added task to your list of ways to keep your household chores and your responsibilities for your children mapped out. Next, we will discuss **sustaining your real friends**.

CHAPTER 6

Where are Those Friends?

Did you notice that you started hanging out less with your single friends once married? Did you notice that many married couples tend to hang out with other friends that are married? Did you see that you tend to hang out with other married people with kids once you had kids? Get ready. Many people experience less time spent with these friends who are married once they state they are getting a divorce. You may have some that will still be there, but many experience a loss. I am not sure what it is. It might be that they are worried they are next or that it is contagious. Maybe they don't know who to invite or get too involved and take sides. That is okay because guess who you will find? Your friends that you made before you met your soon-to-be-ex. Reach out to them. Most likely, they will be glad to hear from you and would love to catch up with you. You are going to want to **sustain your real friends**.

For me, my kids went to a private school. It was a bit awkward because no one there that I knew of had been divorced. Imagine a party with all the married couples and you, the soon-to-be divorcee. Perhaps it was in my head but maybe not. People can be polite but judge you in the back of their heads. Hey, at least they were polite. Another time I decided to drop the kids at the party and was asked, "Where do you think you are going?" I think it was a little bit of jealousy. Maybe she thought I was going out on a date. Everyone has their preference for a group of how many friends. Some have a ton of friends but most likely only have a few really close to them. I know a lot of people but have a few very close friends. Selective perhaps. Shouldn't you somewhat be? Keep reaching out, joining groups, and trying different activities. You will find some you will click with, and you will know it, and it will be great.

Your married friends that continued to reach out to you are golden. They will be there and most likely stay friends with each of you as well. These people generally are the ones that have a strong marriage, not worried about your divorce being contagious, or you sweeping up their spouse.

Your friends may listen to some of your complaints about the divorce. Be careful because they may also be friends with your ex. I urge you to get a counselor to tell all the stuff you need to work on and leave your friends to do something fun. Did you move out of state and want more friends? Pick up some hobbies you like to improve on and perhaps join some organizations, clubs, or get-togethers. You could look through the Meetup app. Money is tight, and you need a counselor and not be the sobbing mess in front of your friends? There is 7cups.com with unrestricted access to trained volunteers offering non-therapeutic advice. If you need further professional help, you can upgrade your membership to a licensed therapist. Your local church may also have services. Also, try the *Talkspace Therapy and Counseling* app.

Having friends makes everything better. Friends help to enjoy the good times even more so and make the difficult times a little easier. You won't be so isolated when you have close friends. A workout buddy that keeps you accountable can help you achieve those physical and mental benefits discussed in Chapter 4. If you are having difficulty with friends, there are podcasts that can help improve your friendships such as the *Friend Forward* podcast. Do you already have one friend? It is a good idea to have a few. What if something happens to your one friend? It is good to have another one, as well. I think too often people tell themselves the wrong thing: "I reached out, and they did not respond" and then give up. Maybe they do not have the time right now, but in the future, they will. Worst-case scenario, let's say you rub them the wrong way, and they don't want to hang out with you. It is okay. There are plenty of others that will. If you think not, ask why. Maybe once you stop worrying about yourself so much and focus on others, you will feel better. All you need to be saying is, next. The sales people who make the most money also tend to have the most no's. The ones with the most friends are the ones that reached out the most, and it was over time they built that group of friends. Close friends are good, and having light talk acquaintances is excellent too.

Great friends listen and schedule a time to connect. They go out of their way to help each other. Building these skills will bring more joy to your world. Avoiding meeting others for possible friendships just prolongs your agony of wanting to connect. What is it that you are passionate about? Try different things. Some things will work out, and some things might not, and that is okay. I remember I started taking flute lessons. I took them for several years but played by myself, not in a band. I attempted to be part of a jazz band. They were very kind, but I was out of my league. With no other flute players, it was up to me to figure out where I come in and with so much going on, counting notes and getting in at the right place was stressful. When I finally got some of the songs under my belt, they picked up new pieces to start. I realized I can enjoy listening to the band instead of being in the band. Playing the flute was giving me pain in my neck and shoulder anyways. Some day if there is a beginner's jazz band that will include the flute, maybe I'll reconsider. For now, I am genuinely enjoying my local Toastmaster's group and hiking or wine tasting with some friends. The point is to find out what it is that you are passionate about and look for ways to learn more about that topic.

Inviting friends and have them bring a friend or two is another great way to meet more people. You never know what might intrigue you and get your mind to start daydreaming about the possibilities of the future. Recently I was invited to wine tasting, and my friend asked her friend. Lacy was previously divorced, and years later, she is engaged. The two of them have a home in the wine country and a home in the south of France. I listened to her story about how they decided to move and retire there eventually. It gave me a glimpse of new possibilities and adventures. I truly enjoyed the stories. Traveling to the different wineries of course, topped it all off.

Are you self-employed? Have you considered joining a local Business Network International group? I have to say I have been self-employed for almost three decades, and I joined during the pandemic. I have signed up as one of the growth and events leaders. That would not be my typical choice. But you know what? I am enjoying it very much. It forces me to figure out what others like to do and invest some time in making it happen. When you are one of the event coordinators, you will show up and stop making excuses about why you can't go. This will allow you to explore different places with an open mind. Recently we went to a dispensary. You know what, a lot of people came to see what it is all about. It was great to hear that it is a family-run business and listen to the story about the Dad and both sons and their previous background. I was amazed to hear what it takes to get something like that up and running.

Get inspired. What is it that you are doing right now to help people? What can you do to get involved more if you aren't already? Do you have a skill that others could benefit from? Maybe you know how to crochet. You know what? That is a great skill to have, and the meditative nature of the task allows you to focus on that and your mind can stop repeatedly ruminating, for instance, about the divorce. There are a lot of people who would love to learn this skill! I know many of these types of skills get lost through the generations. However, many want that skill back—what a lovely gift to give to your close friends or your children.

Maybe you have never had the time to learn how to cook. Take some time and invest in a cooking class or learn some new recipes and perhaps some pastries or bread. Get great at one of these items, and then share with your friends and look how that blossoms. One of my friends, who recently passed away, would always make these Krostule pastries during the holidays. It was such a nice gesture. And I have to be honest - by the time I came home from picking them up, there were only maybe one or two remaining for my daughters. I had eaten the rest! She touched her friends and family with her kind gestures in so many ways. Her taking time to make a special homemade treat made you feel special. I realized that is something I could do more. Get good at making one item and sharing it with others more often. It is true, though, when it is delicious, it can be hard not to eat them all yourself! Or consider making that perfect-because-you-made-it scarf to give away. You are building dear friendships and building your value when you see them wearing it and how they tell everyone you made it for them and how nice it is. The activity doesn't have to be expensive, for instance like golfing or skiing. You could learn something online and then share your talent with others too. The point is we all have skills, and if you feel you don't, find some. What do others comment to you about what you are great at? Perhaps it could start where you are meeting others doing a physical activity. Going for a hike, a run, yoga, or lifting weights with a friend will mentally and physically make you accountable and help you healthily build more substantial esteem. Perhaps you like to join a co-ed soccer team, kick the ball around and have some fun. There are so many choices. If the kids are with you, it will be more difficult to make the vital time for yourself, but you can easily find something to do when they are at their activities. You have to carve out the time for yourself. Otherwise, it simply will not happen at all.

CHAPTER 7

Where are My Goggles?

When you are in a daring divorce, it is like being in a time tunnel. To get through it can help to have some **tunnel vision**. To stay focused, you will have a much easier time accepting what is instead of what it was in the past. You need to be present to what is. Some people going through the divorce live in the past. For instance, anything that their partner did, for instance, let's say they were silent if mad at you, you then perceive anyone silent to you is giving you the same treatment and is mad at you. Or, if your spouse had an affair, you consistently feel that your future love will do the same. Or maybe you are one living in the future instead of dealing with the current situation. You go on a date when you are not ready and start telling your date, "Oh, I have three kids, but you and I could have one more and start making plans." Going from one box right into another box does not give you time to accept what is going on and why it is going on.

You need to learn from your experiences, and taking the knowledge to your future by practicing living in the moment by accepting the moment will help you stay focused and heal. Keep your eyes on the present moment. It is like the year 2020. It hits, and your life can seem to be crazy. Similar to swimming from Alcatraz to San Francisco in the bay waters. If you are not wearing your goggles, you can get a lot of saltwater in them. It can burn. If you swim and keep only taking your breath on one side and not looking straight ahead, you may find yourself drifting far off to the side. Looking both ways and looking straight ahead is ideal. That way, you know if you are too far off from the center. Some people will start to spin, but fortunately, they spin down like a corkscrew and make it to the other side. Others, unfortunately, do not look at the end of the tunnel; instead, they run around like a mouse on a wheel that keeps spinning but doesn't get anywhere.

The ones who get to the end of the tunnel through the storm use the B.E.S.T tips. You need to stay focused no matter how challenging the circumstances are. If you want the divorce and thinking your spouse will go with you to file the papers and come up with an agreement together by mediation, that would be fantastic. Some file the paperwork and hope all will go through with mediation and come to an agreement. Unfortunately, many partners are hurt and protective of what they see as not yours but only their own. The party will flat out tell you it's not going to be easy. If you want the divorce, do you think your partner should have to figure out how to file the papers when your partner doesn't want it? If you no longer see yourself with this person, why are you waiting? It isn't easy, and at times, it can seem unsurmountable on how to figure out how to manage it all. If your spouse is not agreeable to go to mediation how long are you going to wait to figure it out yourself or get help with an attorney? If you are wanting the divorce ultimately, it will be up to you to file the papers. It is easier to get the papers filed with an attorney, but some don't have the extra funds. You can go on YouTube, and it will walk you through it. The point is to get started. If something isn't right with the papers, the court will tell you what is wrong and what you need to fix. At least you have started through the tunnel. Just talking about it or wanting it is not going to get you there. If you no longer see yourself with this person, why are you waiting? It isn't easy, and at times, it can seem unsurmountable on how to figure out how to manage it all.

Get over the fact that your soon-to-be-ex may never have liked your kids being in all the activities you signed them up for and will now refuse to help pick them up or help you out with rides, etc. If you think your soon-to-be-ex should help out with you taking care of your parents or your side of the family responsibilities, why? Because of the kids? They do not see eye to eye with you. Otherwise, they would be cooperating. Unreasonable? That is in the eyes of the beholder. Trust me. They think you are unreasonable. No one wants to hear it. Do yourself a favor, start acting as if they are not available, period. See how you can manage. Maybe neither of you is willing to move out of the house. Perhaps figure out how your kids can share the master bedroom, and you each get your own room until you can get the house sold or one of you move out. It is essential to look at your state and get advice on leaving or moving out of the home, especially if you own it. the party not wanting the divorce will thrive on you getting upset and making it difficult. By now, you should have a bank account that only you can access. Maybe your ex has left the house and suddenly turned off the utilities if they were in their name. Maybe they will start trying to sell off all of their goods.

Something I am good at is listening to the divorce attorney. She asked me, "Do you want this to be as simple as possible, so you get to the end of the tunnel and through the storm, or do you want to drag it out?" Be more than reasonable. Show on the papers that it would be easier just to sign it. After the divorce, even though we had shared custody, I ended up having my girls all of the time. Yes, I could have fought for financial support to prove the other party could provide it, but I didn't because I am too busy making my own business grow. I see it as his loss. I could have put a lien on his items. But why? Is it worth the stress? These items deter you from getting to the end of the tunnel. Having a good divorce attorney will tell you right off if it is worth your effort or not to seek or go after another party. In my opinion, the best thing to do is to pray for the other party to get their life together, and maybe someday they will see it is unfortunate they did not want to provide for their kids. They may say I support them in other ways. I did not push further or argue over what the other party should do. My family does not live in the area. But I have great ex-in-laws that I still consider part of the family. It is a blessing that they still celebrate the holidays and special occasions altogether with my children. Had I fought all the other stuff out, would that be the case? You will have to weigh that out. My girls' Dad is their Dad, and he has amazing talents that I hope wear off on my girls. Pray that they get the best of both of us and figure out the rest for themselves. What can keep you from getting to the end of the tunnel? Are you bickering over who gets what? Remember, you can't take it to the grave. Businesses, homes, money, if it doesn't end up in your pocket or shared with you, hopefully it will eventually go to your kids. If it doesn't, that is quite spiteful. Sickening.

When the other party starts kicking and screaming and saying mean things to others or your kids, bite your tongue. All of the smart people can see right through it, and if your kids do not, they will in time. Stay focused. What is it that you want? Has someone said something to you or your children, and now you are all wound up ready to start a fight? Chill out. Go for a walk. Heck, go out for a run or maybe a bike ride, or hit some tennis balls. Maybe go for a swim. Swimming helps relax you and helps you get your breath back and stay calm. Maybe you need to listen better to your attorney. What did they tell you to do? Have you done it? What about your counselor? Are you listening to them and actively doing what they ask? Listening and doing are two completely different things. Get off your butt and do what you are supposed to do, like what your attorney, counselor, and these B.E.S.T. tips recommend for you.

If you are spinning out of control and not getting anywhere, ask yourself, what is a big problem people have with a divorce? They are either continue to live in the past or live in the future. You need to be in the present moment. You need to make a habit of accepting what is.

Be busy and productive. What are you doing right now to obtain the other goals in your life currently? Do you have deadlines? Maybe if you have too much time on your hands, perhaps make those deadlines a little sooner. Do you still have not enough on your to-do list? If you are arguing back and forth with your soon-to-be-ex, then clearly, you do not have enough to do. It would help if YOU were BUSY, not with mundane items but building blocks to building your character. Maybe you could sign up for a running event. You could set up a meetup group and be the person in charge. Perhaps starting a podcast on a subject you are passionate about. Maybe you need to start learning how to play an instrument or helping another friend or family with things that need help in their home. When you get yourself off of the wheel, you can see more clearly. If you start eating and learning new recipes for the new you and exercising, these are all items building your character. Maybe you can write in a journal and someday publish your book.

Expect nothing. Are you going around and around in a wheel because you are expecting something? Remember, expect nothing. Ask for all you want but expect nothing. That includes them continuing to help take your in-laws or cousins, etc., on your side to their activities. The plan is that them helping out with this is not going to happen. Is this why you are getting dizzy because you are not getting what you want? Stop saying he should or she should be doing this or that. The answer is you should expect nothing. Perhaps this is the better way to get through life in general.

Are you spinning? Keep it up, and you will see that your friends turn away from you. STOP. Want to help yourself? **Sustain your real friends**. Listen to your friends and what is going on in their life, which will help you relax a bit. Life isn't all about you. It is about making life better for those around you. Getting a divorce when the relationship has ended is better than continuing to pretend all is okay in make-believe land. You will age quite quickly if you keep fighting. Meet up with new people and invest time in friendships. Maybe there is meetup support for women going through a divorce or men going through divorce near you.

Are you spinning? How do you want to get through the divorce? Spin like a corkscrew, mouse on a wheel, or keep steady and focused and swim out of the storm to land? Your peace of mind depends on how you choose to handle this situation. You can build your character here or tear yourself apart. You can be the person who contributes to their fellow man by taking better care of themselves and living life, not pretending all is okay but finding and discovering themselves to live life fully and be available for the next love, the next adventure. You show your family if one of the partners wants out how to do it maturely, even if the other party chooses to divorce differently. **Tunnel vision** in the time tunnel will help you keep your eyes on the sunshine. Do you want to stay in the storm? Do you like the waves coming up over your head and then getting tumbled to the bottom of the sea? Or would you prefer to be able to ride on top of the waves, steadily making progress to the land with the sun and calm waters? YOU can do this daring divorce and navigate the storm with the B.E.S.T. tips.

CHAPTER 8

Story of Julia

In the story of Julia, you will see how one learns to accept what is and how one can make use of the B.E.S.T. tips. Julia married her school sweetheart. They ended up living in a beautiful home in a great neighborhood. They had eight children, five boys and three girls. All was great, except the wife felt neglected. Her husband, Steve, spent all of his time working. He would make occasional comments about how good-looking someone was, and that would hurt her feelings. She began to eat more and more to soothe her pain of being stuck at home with the children with no adult interaction. She loved being a Mom, but she wanted to be the wife her husband would adore and make time to spend with her. Steve was tired of hearing her complain about him not working in the house or not being able to help with kids' activities or ever doing anything with her. She felt like Peggy in the T.V. show sitcom *Married...With Children.* The kids wondered why their Dad did not attend their events. He would take time to even travel to other countries to find quality products for his company. She was grateful to have beautiful kids and a lovely home, but she honestly preferred a smaller home where it wasn't so stressful for her husband to provide for the family. She did not want to stress about not running the air conditioner because it would cost too much. She saw that if others asked her husband to help them get something to work, he often would help out just by being a nice person. But when she asked for the same, he would reply "Not now." Unless painstaking constant bickering got him to budge, he would say, "I will do it, but don't push me to do it."

Years would go by, and the issues stayed the same. He would jump for his clients, but he would constantly put her requests for help at home aside. She used to make dinner but now would not put any special effort into it as she often ate alone with her children, and he would come home late. They eventually ended up sleeping in different rooms. She did not greet him like she once did. Instead, when he came home, she often left to get some of her own time. Julia would go to the club and spend time in the sauna to getaway. The business was going well until there was the 2008 financial recession. Contracts and scheduled orders were canceled. The husband explained to Julia that the lifestyle they have been living will have to pause and that she will need to work. She was frustrated; you will take the luxuries I have away when the real luxury I would want would be to spend time together, and that is going to be even less than what it is now? She found work, yet she also found attention from another man. Someone who made her feel beautiful and loved and cherished; something she was yearning to have from her husband.

Julia did not want to continue living in a lie and pursued a divorce. She accepted that her wanting to have the fancy lifestyle was nice, but she was not happy being with a man who never spent time with her. Steve was devastated. He thought his wife would always be there. He accepted the fact that he took her for granted, and this was a mistake. He wanted to make it work out. She was not willing to budge. She was done with the marriage. He accepted the reality that the marriage was over with Julia not wanting to continue. She realized her part in the divorce. Both parties realized they needed to work to have two separate households. Although they fought to keep the house, the house ultimately became Julia's in the final agreement. He was bitter but then able to turn it around by accepting what was, accepting that finally, the house will be his children's, which gave him peace of mind. He prayed for all parties and especially prayed for his children to be happy. Each spouse stayed busy. One with work and writing and the other with work, playing soccer, and helping out with community organizations. Both parties asked for stuff. Neither one got all they wanted, but both learned to be happy when the other would contribute. Both parties lost contact with several of their friends and nourished new relationships with others and built on their old friendships before their marriage.

When Julia felt herself spinning, she learned to step away and stay calm. She noticed that if she did not make comments, he eventually stopped harassing her. Realizing that he could not get her to react helped him to realize he lost her. Julia and her husband recognized their marriage as having been on a train with upset and lack of fulfillment as the final destination. They discovered one could get off it at any time and get on another train like a happy train. Julia learned that being uncomfortable caused her to grow. With hypnosis, she was able to see what she could not change. Julia learned how to be grateful for having such wonderful, beautiful kids. Making her hypnosis recording, she discovered more confidence in being able to follow through with her decision. She developed inner strength.

Steve did not want the divorce but kept in mind the *Serenity Prayer*, a prayer written by the American theologian Reinhold Niebuhr.

God, grant me the serenity to accept the things
I cannot change,
courage to change the things I can,
and wisdom to know the difference.

When he observed that he could not change that his spouse wanted a divorce, he had an easier time accepting it and carrying on.

Going through a divorce, many avoid dealing with it and keep putting it off for as long as possible. They rent a one-bedroom even if they have kids because they think it will only be temporary. They prolong the action that one needs to do to move on because they do not want to accept what is. Instead, accept what is by using visualization. For instance, imagine that today you're dealing with the stress of the divorce. You have all your documents – all your feelings – in a box put in a locked file cabinet. You place this box in your car, and you take it to the conference room overlooking the ocean at a fancy hotel. You have this room reserved just for you for as long as you need to observe each document. Take all of these documents and place each individually on the conference table. One by one, put these documents into their appropriate file. Where does it belong? There are file folders and a sharpie pen on the table. Label your files, your feelings as you go along. Notice they are there. Acknowledge each of these feelings in each of the documents, the wrongs, and the rights. Take as long as you need. Some of your labels may be resentment, frustration, fear, heaviness, excitement, and relief. There are most likely many feelings happening all at the same time.

Once all your forms are in their appropriate file, you acknowledge their presence and notice a sense of relief. You see things as they are and what needs to be done to move to the next chapter of your life. You can place these files all organized back into your box, and you can return to it anytime you like. As you walk over to the window, you see the beautiful ocean crashing on the beach and the beautiful sun shining down with birds flying. You leave the conference room, walk down the pathway over to the edge of the ocean and walk barefoot, getting your calves wet. Then, you decide to walk further into the sea and go for a swim. It is a little cold but most refreshing. Like one that finishes their taxes, you feel good about getting it processed. Maybe it will cost you, but you feel relieved it has been dealt with and is not all scattered and thrown in a box. Your thoughts are organized and, by filing them into their appropriate file, have been received and acknowledged.

Would you like to make self-recorded hypnosis for acceptance? Record this hypnosis script for yourself and listen to it daily or go to www.DaringDivorce.com for a free downloadable audible version.

> *Inside of us, we have the most helpful answers. You have all that you need to make yourself feel at ease. If you need to readjust your seat, cushion, or pillow, you can do so at any time.*
>
> *I am going to make some suggestions to help you relax. Start relaxing by closing your eyes. If you notice any specific parts of you that*

have been holding tension in your body, go ahead and relax those muscles. Release any stress that you are having.

Have you noticed your breaths are becoming slower? This is good. Take a deep breath through your nose

for 1, 2, 3, 4,

hold for 1, 2, 3, 4,

and exhale through your mouth

for 1, 2, 3, 4.

Imagine the muscle of your temples relaxing, the forehead, the brows, and jaw fully released of tension.

Feel the pressure in the neck across the shoulder down the arms and hands leaving your body.

It is okay if your mind wanders a bit. Just continue to relax the muscles of your back, buttocks, thigh, calf, and feet.

Release any tension that you have in your chest or stomach.

Feel the tension being release through our body like dew escaping the grass on the edge of the river.

You feel so relaxed like your muscles are in total limp. You feel restful. Any remaining tension sees it finally escaping your body. Bring in yourself deeper with the sense of being at a state of being relaxed.

You realize it was not so difficult to relax your body, and you notice that relaxing your body likewise your mind follows through and relaxes. At this point, you feel so good. You realize that you could open your eyes up if needed, but it feels so closed you just keep them closed. You are content with this feeling. As your body becomes even more relaxed, you realize you have the skill of being able to control your body and your mind.

Imagine yourself at the top of a mountain at an overlook.

You see ten steps down the pathway to a beautiful river that overlooks the valley below.

You go to the top step.

Imagine you moving from one step to the next, and with each step down, you become more relaxed.

91

In fact, ten times more relaxed with each step down.

Moving from the ninth to the eighth step

From the eighth step to the seventh

Relaxing more, letting your mind wander and body relax

From the seventh to the sixth

From the sixth to the fifth

You feel so relaxed

From the fifth to the fourth

Getting closer

Doubling the relaxation

Complete calmness

From the fourth to the third

Three

Two

One

You can see the bottom step. With the next step, you are going to lay on the most comfortable full-size raft that has a beautiful cushioned top. You lay on it

Zero

As you lay on the raft, you feel so light and relaxed as the raft gently starts to travel in the calm river. As you lay on the raft, you notice your mind open to new ideas and experiences and accept what is.

As you travel down this river on the raft, all is good. You reflect on the great things in your life as the river continues on the current gets more intense, and there are some big rocks and some fallen trees you reflect and notice some of the more challenging times that you have in your life.

You may not like the fact you have to go through this terrain on the raft or the challenges occurring in your life, but you accept it. You are there, and you grab the rower and start your way through the raft to make it to the other area where you can see the water is calm once again. You are doing great. You stay calm and figure out the best way to make it to the calm waters.

We do not have to give up the experiences you have shared but look forward to your next adventures in life. You have many strengths and talents, and you can use them to move forward in your life productively.

You are getting yourself ready and magnetizing yourself to beautiful, loving relationships. This is amazing. In just a short time, you have accepted what is and can look forward to what is to come. You acknowledge you are in some tricky waters, but soon you will get out of it and have learned from this experience.

You may help others with what you have learned to help them get through similar challenges.

What are your top three talents?

When you open your eyes, write these three talents down somewhere you can see them often.

Remember that these talents will help you get to the calm waters as you carry on your day.

Imagine you have made it to the other side. You get to the land. You stretch.

You become more alert and excited with each step up.

10, 9, 8 muscle waking up,

7, 6, 5 looking forward to sharing your talents with others,

4, 3, 2, 1 open your eyes.
Take a deep breath in, exhale, fully alert and
awake, feeling great about having accepted
the challenges in life.

Another thing that could help is to write at night before you go to bed any issues troubling you at night before you sleep. You might find an answer in your dream when you wake up if you recall and write it down. You might find your answer hidden in your subconscious mind that makes you aware of your dream. For additional information on this read, *Wake Up to Your Dreams* by Justina Lasley.

CHAPTER 9

Daring Divorce Promise

I f after reading this book and completing the suggested exercises and practicing the B.E.S.T. tips you still want to make your marriage work, fantastic. Remember, it takes both parties to want that, and if that is the case, I wish you success. However, if you are in the situation where "like it or not" the divorce is going to happen, then

I promise that you, too, can get through it and at the same time be building your character. If you apply what you have read in this book, you will find that you could get through the divorce with your dignity still at hand. Remember, if you were wronged, most likely the other party was too. Start your day praying for the soon-to-be-ex, yourself, your kids, and whoever else involved to be happy and kind. Going through life knowing that people come together to have kids in some marriages, some marriages succeed, and others do not work out. It is all okay. We live, we learn, we grow. Maybe, initially you want to pretend all was okay, but you and all around you knew it was not okay. You are not the one that played it safe and pretended all was okay. You took the opportunity for a daring divorce, the opportunity to live authentically in search of your true self.

As you are going through the divorce, remember the B.E.S.T. tips.

Be busy by being productive

Expect nothing

Sustain your real friends

Tunnel vision for the time tunnel

What else will you add to your plate? Being busy with being productive and establishing deadlines will help you not dwell on the side effects of the divorce. So you will find yourself busy with your activities and you will process the divorce in bits instead of being consumed entirely with it all day and night long because you have other stuff that makes up your day and your thoughts. Imagine someone drinking and only drinking with no food or someone who may drink but takes food with their drink and takes sips instead of taking it all in. The ones who didn't take other items into their system like food become drunk and miserable. You will find yourself sharpening up on the talents you already have or learning new things to do, and discovering what you would like to seek more knowledge to develop your unique talent.

If you go through the divorce process by expecting nothing, you will be prepared to sustain yourself and your family and be pleasantly surprised if you get what you asked for. What you will find is much better than always living with the expectation that "he should do this" or "she should do that". If you expect nothing, you won't be so upset and bitter. It's just like republicans versus democrats. The democrats should do this, or the republicans should do that. It solves nothing. You want something done, get used to being more self-sufficient, and be amazed at the things you can do on your own.

Sustaining your real friends or making some new ones you will find will help you grow your unique character and provide the support you need to help you in the next chapter in your life. Setting in your schedule to meet with your friends monthly will help you stay calm and connected with a group supporting you.

Having tunnel vision for the time tunnel will help you get through the divorce without getting significantly dizzy or being tossed and turned upside down and around. Instead, it will help you keep traction in moving forward and on to your next adventure.

So when are you going to begin? What other items will you be adding to your to-do list of being busy and productive? What is something new? What physical activity do you want to partake in or accomplish? Will you be taking up knitting, or will you join a Toastmasters group or a Rotary Club? Maybe a musical instrument you want to polish up on or a foreign language you've always wanted to learn?

What are the things you think he or she should do? How can you turn it around by considering, "Although it would be nice, I don't expect him to do this, so I will instead do this"? What would that look like? Would it be you going to school? Would it be making arrangements for someone else to help pick up the kids after school? Would it mean you would have to make additional income if you want your children to continue activities that your partner never wants them to be involved in? How are you planning on earning extra income and or being more frugal?

Who do you want to remain friends with and who in your past would you like to reconnect with? What type of friends do you want to be hanging out with? Do you want to be hanging out with the hypocrites who judge you but can't see the log in their own eyes? For every verse in the bible to stay married, I can find verses giving reasons acceptable for divorce. There will be judgers. Don't worry about them. Their time is coming where they may reach out to you for support.

When you notice that you are spinning from comments, how will you keep your tunnel vision? Will you have a divorce coach or a group of friends going through similar stuff? Are there specific breathing techniques you will learn and practice? Meditation? Prayer? Maybe hypnosis to help reduce stress. What will be your reminder to put those goggles back on correctly and perhaps a little bit tighter? How will you adjust those earplugs so you do not hear all that is being said?

What will you do? I promise that if you do even one of these items from the B.E.S.T. tips, your divorce will go through easier. If you do all the B.E.S.T. tips, you will be amazed at how much you accomplished and the character you build, and the character you help make in your children. Life is an adventure, not meant to be stagnant, but meant to continue evolving and growing to be the person God designed you to be.

SOURCES

Claudia Hammond
Why your brain likes it when you multitask
MEDICAL MYTHS | HEALTH February 19 2016
https://www.bbc.com/future/article/20160218-
why-multi-tasking-might-not-be-such-a-bad-idea

Journal Frontiers in Aging and Neuroscience
(August 25, 2015)

How to Relieve Stress with Art Therapy
By Elizabeth Scott, MS
Reviewed by Amy Morin, L.C.S.W. on
January 24, 2020
https://www.verywellmind.com/art-therapy-
relieve-stress-by-being-creative-3144581

Kaimal G, Ray K, Muniz J. Reduction of Cortisol Levels and Participants' Responses Following Art Making. Art Ther (Alex). 2016;33(2):74-80. doi:10.1080/07421656.2016.1166832

Sansone RA, et al. (2013). Sunshine, serotonin, and skin: A partial explanation for seasonal patterns in psychopathology? ncbi.nlm.nih.gov/pmc/articles/PMC3779905/

The Women's Institute for a Secure Retirement reports

How to accept things as they are
(without giving up)
by MoretoMum | January 7, 2019 | Life, Mindset, Self Care

Richard Nongard's Big Book of Hypnosis Scripts How to Create Lasting Change Using Contextual Hypnotherapy, Mindfulness Meditation and Hypnotic Phenomena by Richard K. Nongard, 2018

To access a FREE recorded hypnosis script to help you with acceptance, to book Stacey Duckett to speak at your upcoming event or to have her as a guest on a podcast go to www.DaringDivorce.com.

Many people going through a divorce can find difficulty with sleeping. If that is you, check out her other book *Sensational Sleep*. Better Sleep for a Better You!

www.ingramcontent.com/pod-product-compliance
Lightning Source LLC
Chambersburg PA
CBHW060119050426
42448CB00010B/1937